This]
Belongs To:

MW01164631

Walk, Hike, Camp, & Sightseeing

Date: _____ Weather: _____

Start Time: _____Time End: _____
Total Time: _____Distance: _____
Elevation: _____
Walk/Hike Trail Type: _____

Rate The Walk/Hike/Camp ✿ ✿ ✿ ✿ ✿

City/State: _____
Trail Name/s: _____
Terrain: _____
Phone Reception: | YES | NO |
First Visit ✿   Return Visit ✿

Companion/s: _____
_____

Bathroom? Water?: _____

Observances of Interest: _____
_____
_____
_____
_____

Things To Bring: _____
_____
_____

Notes For Next Time: _____
_____
_____

Notes & Journaling

Images Or Drawing

Walk, Hike, Camp, & Sightseeing

Date: _____ Weather: _____

Start Time: _____ Time End: _____
Total Time: _____ Distance: _____
Elevation: _____
Walk/Hike Trail Type: _____

Rate The Walk/Hike/Camp ✿ ✿ ✿ ✿ ✿

City/State: _____
Trail Name/s: _____
Terrain: _____
Phone Reception: | YES | | NO |
First Visit ✿ Return Visit ✿

Companion/s: _____
_____

Bathroom? Water?: _____

Observances of Interest: _____
_____
_____
_____
_____

Things To Bring: _____
_____
_____

Notes For Next Time: _____
_____
_____

Notes & Journaling

_____
_____
_____
_____
_____
_____
_____
_____
_____
_____
_____
_____

Images Or Drawing

Walk, Hike, Camp, & Sightseeing

Date: _____ Weather: _____

Start Time: _____Time End: _____
Total Time: _____Distance: _____
Elevation: _____
Walk/Hike Trail Type: _____

Rate The Walk/Hike/Camp ✿ ✿ ✿ ✿ ✿

City/State: _____
Trail Name/s: _____
Terrain: _____
Phone Reception: | YES | | NO |
First Visit ✿   Return Visit ✿

Companion/s: _____
_____

Bathroom? Water?: _____

Observances of Interest: _____
_____
_____
_____
_____

Things To Bring: _____
_____
_____

Notes For Next Time: _____
_____
_____

Notes & Journaling

_____
_____
_____
_____
_____
_____
_____
_____
_____
_____
_____
_____
_____

Images Or Drawing

Walk, Hike, Camp, & Sightseeing

Date: Weather:

Start Time: _____ Time End: _____
Total Time: _____ Distance: _____
Elevation: _____
Walk/Hike Trail Type: _____

Rate The Walk/Hike/Camp ✿ ✿ ✿ ✿ ✿

City/State: _____
Trail Name/s: _____
Terrain: _____
Phone Reception: | YES | | NO |
First Visit ✿   Return Visit ✿

Companion/s: _____
_____

Bathroom? Water?: _____

Observances of Interest: _____
_____
_____
_____
_____

Things To Bring: _____
_____
_____

Notes For Next Time: _____
_____
_____

Notes & Journaling

_____
_____
_____
_____
_____
_____
_____
_____
_____
_____
_____
_____
_____

Images Or Drawing

Walk, Hike, Camp, & Sightseeing

Date: Weather:

Start Time: _____ Time End: _____
Total Time: _____ Distance: _____
Elevation: _____
Walk/Hike Trail Type: _____

Rate The Walk/Hike/Camp   ✿ ✿ ✿ ✿ ✿

City/State: _____
Trail Name/s: _____
Terrain: _____
Phone Reception: | YES | | NO |
First Visit ✿   Return Visit ✿

Companion/s: _____
_____

Bathroom? Water?: _____

Observances of Interest: _____
_____
_____
_____
_____

Things To Bring: _____
_____
_____

Notes For Next Time: _____
_____
_____

Notes & Journaling

Images Or Drawing

Walk, Hike, Camp, & Sightseeing

Date: Weather:

Start Time: _____ Time End: _____
Total Time: _____ Distance: _____
Elevation: _____
Walk/Hike Trail Type: _____

Rate The Walk/Hike/Camp ✿ ✿ ✿ ✿ ✿

City/State: _____
Trail Name/s: _____
Terrain: _____
Phone Reception: | YES | | NO |
First Visit ✿   Return Visit ✿

Companion/s: _____
_____

Bathroom? Water?: _____

Observances of Interest: _____
_____
_____
_____
_____

Things To Bring: _____
_____
_____

Notes For Next Time: _____
_____
_____

Notes & Journaling

_____
_____
_____
_____
_____
_____
_____
_____
_____
_____
_____
_____
_____
_____

Images Or Drawing

Walk, Hike, Camp, & Sightseeing

Date: Weather:

Start Time: _____ Time End: _____
Total Time: _____ Distance: _____
Elevation: _____
Walk/Hike Trail Type: _____

Rate The Walk/Hike/Camp   ✿ ✿ ✿ ✿ ✿

City/State: _____
Trail Name/s: _____
Terrain: _____
Phone Reception: | YES | | NO |
First Visit ✿   Return Visit   ✿

Companion/s: _____
_____

Bathroom? Water?: _____

Observances of Interest: _____
_____
_____
_____
_____

Things To Bring: _____
_____
_____

Notes For Next Time: _____
_____
_____

Notes & Journaling

_____
_____
_____
_____
_____
_____
_____
_____
_____
_____
_____
_____

Images Or Drawing

Walk, Hike, Camp, & Sightseeing

Date: _____ Weather: _____

Start Time: _____ Time End: _____
Total Time: _____ Distance: _____
Elevation: _____
Walk/Hike Trail Type: _____

Rate The Walk/Hike/Camp ✿ ✿ ✿ ✿ ✿

City/State: _____
Trail Name/s: _____
Terrain: _____
Phone Reception: | YES | | NO |
First Visit ✿   Return Visit ✿

Companion/s: _____
_____

Bathroom? Water?: _____

Observances of Interest: _____
_____
_____
_____
_____

Things To Bring: _____
_____
_____

Notes For Next Time: _____
_____
_____

Notes & Journaling

Images Or Drawing

Walk, Hike, Camp, & Sightseeing

Date: Weather:

Start Time: _____ Time End: _____
Total Time: _____ Distance: _____
Elevation: _____
Walk/Hike Trail Type: _____

Rate The Walk/Hike/Camp ✿ ✿ ✿ ✿ ✿

City/State: _____
Trail Name/s: _____
Terrain: _____
Phone Reception: | YES | | NO |
First Visit ✿   Return Visit ✿

Companion/s: _____
_____

Bathroom? Water?: _____

Observances of Interest: _____
_____
_____
_____
_____

Things To Bring: _____
_____

Notes For Next Time: _____
_____
_____

Notes & Journaling

_____
_____
_____
_____
_____
_____
_____
_____
_____
_____
_____
_____
_____

Images Or Drawing

Walk, Hike, Camp, & Sightseeing

Date: Weather:

Start Time: _____ Time End: _____
Total Time: _____ Distance: _____
Elevation: _____
Walk/Hike Trail Type: _____

Rate The Walk/Hike/Camp ✸ ✸ ✸ ✸ ✸

City/State: _____
Trail Name/s: _____
Terrain: _____
Phone Reception: | YES | | NO |
First Visit ✿   Return Visit ✿

Companion/s: _____
_____

Bathroom? Water?: _____

Observances of Interest: _____
_____
_____
_____
_____

Things To Bring: _____
_____
_____

Notes For Next Time: _____
_____
_____

Notes & Journaling

Images Or Drawing

Walk, Hike, Camp, & Sightseeing

Date: _____ Weather: _____

Start Time: _____Time End: _____
Total Time: _____Distance: _____
Elevation: _____
Walk/Hike Trail Type: _____

Rate The Walk/Hike/Camp ✿ ✿ ✿ ✿ ✿

City/State: _____
Trail Name/s: _____
Terrain: _____
Phone Reception: | YES | | NO |
First Visit ✿   Return Visit ✿

Companion/s: _____
_____

Bathroom? Water?: _____

Observances of Interest: _____
_____
_____
_____
_____

Things To Bring: _____
_____

Notes For Next Time: _____
_____
_____

Notes & Journaling

_____
_____
_____
_____
_____
_____
_____
_____
_____
_____
_____
_____
_____

Images Or Drawing

Walk, Hike, Camp, & Sightseeing

Date: **Weather:**

Start Time: _____ Time End: _____
Total Time: _____ Distance: _____
Elevation: _____
Walk/Hike Trail Type: _____

Rate The Walk/Hike/Camp   ✿ ✿ ✿ ✿ ✿

City/State: _____
Trail Name/s: _____
Terrain: _____
Phone Reception: | YES | | NO |
First Visit ✿   Return Visit   ✿

Companion/s: _____

_____

Bathroom? Water?: _____

Observances of Interest: _____
_____
_____
_____
_____

Things To Bring: _____
_____
_____

Notes For Next Time: _____
_____
_____

Notes & Journaling

Images Or Drawing

Walk, Hike, Camp, & Sightseeing

Date: **Weather:**

Start Time: _____ Time End: _____
Total Time: _____ Distance: _____
Elevation: _____
Walk/Hike Trail Type: _____

Rate The Walk/Hike/Camp   ✿ ✿ ✿ ✿ ✿

City/State: _____
Trail Name/s: _____
Terrain: _____
Phone Reception: | YES | | NO |
First Visit ✿   Return Visit   ✿

Companion/s: _____

_____

Bathroom? Water?: _____

Observances of Interest: _____

_____
_____
_____
_____

Things To Bring: _____

_____
_____

Notes For Next Time: _____

_____
_____

Notes & Journaling

_____
_____
_____
_____
_____
_____
_____
_____
_____
_____
_____
_____
_____

Images Or Drawing

Walk, Hike, Camp, & Sightseeing

Date: _____ Weather: _____

Start Time: _____ Time End: _____
Total Time: _____ Distance: _____
Elevation: _____
Walk/Hike Trail Type: _____

Rate The Walk/Hike/Camp ✿ ✿ ✿ ✿ ✿

City/State: _____
Trail Name/s: _____
Terrain: _____
Phone Reception: | YES | | NO |
First Visit ✿   Return Visit ✿

Companion/s: _____
_____

Bathroom? Water?: _____

Observances of Interest: _____
_____
_____
_____
_____

Things To Bring: _____
_____
_____

Notes For Next Time: _____
_____
_____

Notes & Journaling

_____
_____
_____
_____
_____
_____
_____
_____
_____
_____
_____
_____
_____

Images Or Drawing

Walk, Hike, Camp, & Sightseeing

Date: _____ Weather: _____

Start Time: _____ Time End: _____
Total Time: _____ Distance: _____
Elevation: _____
Walk/Hike Trail Type: _____

Rate The Walk/Hike/Camp ✿ ✿ ✿ ✿ ✿

City/State: _____
Trail Name/s: _____
Terrain: _____
Phone Reception: | YES | | NO |
First Visit ✿   Return Visit ✿

Companion/s: _____
_____

Bathroom? Water?: _____

Observances of Interest: _____
_____
_____
_____
_____

Things To Bring: _____
_____
_____

Notes For Next Time: _____
_____
_____

Notes & Journaling

Images Or Drawing

Walk, Hike, Camp, & Sightseeing

Date: Weather:

Start Time: _____ Time End: _____
Total Time: _____ Distance: _____
Elevation: _____
Walk/Hike Trail Type: _____

Rate The Walk/Hike/Camp ✿ ✿ ✿ ✿ ✿

City/State: _____
Trail Name/s: _____
Terrain: _____
Phone Reception: | YES | | NO |
First Visit ✿   Return Visit   ✿

Companion/s: _____
_____

Bathroom? Water?: _____

Observances of Interest: _____
_____
_____
_____
_____

Things To Bring: _____
_____
_____

Notes For Next Time: _____
_____
_____

Notes & Journaling

Images Or Drawing

Walk, Hike, Camp, & Sightseeing

Date: Weather:

Start Time: _____ Time End: _____
Total Time: _____ Distance: _____
Elevation: _____
Walk/Hike Trail Type: _____

Rate The Walk/Hike/Camp ✿ ✿ ✿ ✿ ✿

City/State: _____
Trail Name/s: _____
Terrain: _____
Phone Reception: | YES | | NO |
First Visit ✿   Return Visit ✿

Companion/s: _____
_____

Bathroom? Water?: _____

Observances of Interest: _____
_____
_____
_____
_____

Things To Bring: _____
_____
_____

Notes For Next Time: _____
_____
_____

Notes & Journaling

Images Or Drawing

Walk, Hike, Camp, & Sightseeing

Date: _____ Weather: _____

Start Time: _____ Time End: _____
Total Time: _____ Distance: _____
Elevation: _____
Walk/Hike Trail Type: _____

Rate The Walk/Hike/Camp ✿ ✿ ✿ ✿ ✿

City/State: _____
Trail Name/s: _____
Terrain: _____
Phone Reception: | YES | NO |
First Visit ✿   Return Visit ✿

Companion/s: _____
_____

Bathroom? Water?: _____

Observances of Interest: _____
_____
_____
_____
_____

Things To Bring: _____
_____
_____

Notes For Next Time: _____
_____
_____

Notes & Journaling

Images Or Drawing

Walk, Hike, Camp, & Sightseeing

Date: _____ Weather: _____

Start Time: _____Time End: _____
Total Time: _____Distance: _____
Elevation: _____
Walk/Hike Trail Type: _____

Rate The Walk/Hike/Camp ✿ ✿ ✿ ✿ ✿

City/State: _____
Trail Name/s: _____
Terrain: _____
Phone Reception: | YES | | NO |
First Visit ✿   Return Visit ✿

Companion/s: _____
_____

Bathroom? Water?: _____

Observances of Interest: _____
_____
_____
_____
_____

Things To Bring: _____
_____
_____

Notes For Next Time: _____
_____
_____

Notes & Journaling

Images Or Drawing

Walk, Hike, Camp, & Sightseeing

Date: _____ Weather: _____

Start Time: _____ Time End: _____
Total Time: _____ Distance: _____
Elevation: _____
Walk/Hike Trail Type: _____

Rate The Walk/Hike/Camp ✿ ✿ ✿ ✿ ✿

City/State: _____
Trail Name/s: _____
Terrain: _____
Phone Reception: [YES |] [NO |]
First Visit ✿   Return Visit ✿

Companion/s: _____
_____

Bathroom? Water?: _____

Observances of Interest: _____
_____
_____
_____
_____

Things To Bring: _____
_____
_____

Notes For Next Time: _____
_____
_____

Notes & Journaling

Images Or Drawing

Walk, Hike, Camp, & Sightseeing

Date: Weather:

Start Time: _____ Time End: _____
Total Time: _____ Distance: _____
Elevation: _____
Walk/Hike Trail Type: _____

Rate The Walk/Hike/Camp ✿ ✿ ✿ ✿ ✿

City/State: _____
Trail Name/s: _____
Terrain: _____
Phone Reception: | YES | | NO |
First Visit ✿   Return Visit   ✿

Companion/s: _____
_____

Bathroom? Water?: _____

Observances of Interest: _____
_____
_____
_____
_____

Things To Bring: _____
_____
_____

Notes For Next Time: _____
_____
_____

Notes & Journaling

Images Or Drawing

Walk, Hike, Camp, & Sightseeing

Date: Weather:

Start Time: _____ Time End: _____
Total Time: _____ Distance: _____
Elevation: _____
Walk/Hike Trail Type: _____

Rate The Walk/Hike/Camp ✿ ✿ ✿ ✿ ✿

City/State: _____
Trail Name/s: _____
Terrain: _____
Phone Reception: | YES | | NO |
First Visit ✿   Return Visit ✿

Companion/s: _____
_____

Bathroom? Water?: _____

Observances of Interest: _____
_____
_____
_____
_____

Things To Bring: _____
_____
_____

Notes For Next Time: _____
_____
_____

Notes & Journaling

_____
_____
_____
_____
_____
_____
_____
_____
_____
_____
_____
_____

Images Or Drawing

Walk, Hike, Camp, & Sightseeing

Date: Weather:

Start Time: _____ Time End: _____
Total Time: _____ Distance: _____
Elevation: _____
Walk/Hike Trail Type: _____

Rate The Walk/Hike/Camp ✿ ✿ ✿ ✿ ✿

City/State: _____
Trail Name/s: _____
Terrain: _____
Phone Reception: | YES | | NO |
First Visit ✿   Return Visit   ✿

Companion/s: _____
_____

Bathroom? Water?: _____

Observances of Interest: _____
_____
_____
_____
_____

Things To Bring: _____
_____
_____

Notes For Next Time: _____
_____
_____

Notes & Journaling

Images Or Drawing

Walk, Hike, Camp, & Sightseeing

Date: _____ **Weather:** _____

Start Time: _____ Time End: _____
Total Time: _____ Distance: _____
Elevation: _____
Walk/Hike Trail Type: _____

Rate The Walk/Hike/Camp ✿ ✿ ✿ ✿ ✿

City/State: _____
Trail Name/s: _____
Terrain: _____
Phone Reception: | YES | | NO |
First Visit ✿   Return Visit ✿

Companion/s: _____
_____

Bathroom? Water?: _____

Observances of Interest: _____
_____
_____
_____
_____

Things To Bring: _____
_____
_____

Notes For Next Time: _____
_____
_____

Notes & Journaling

_____
_____
_____
_____
_____
_____
_____
_____
_____
_____
_____
_____

Images Or Drawing

Walk, Hike, Camp, & Sightseeing

Date: _____ Weather: _____

Start Time: _____ Time End: _____
Total Time: _____ Distance: _____
Elevation: _____
Walk/Hike Trail Type: _____

Rate The Walk/Hike/Camp ✿ ✿ ✿ ✿ ✿

City/State: _____
Trail Name/s: _____
Terrain: _____
Phone Reception: | YES | | NO |
First Visit ✿   Return Visit ✿

Companion/s: _____
_____

Bathroom? Water?: _____

Observances of Interest: _____
_____
_____
_____
_____

Things To Bring: _____
_____
_____

Notes For Next Time: _____
_____
_____

Notes & Journaling

_____
_____
_____
_____
_____
_____
_____
_____
_____
_____
_____
_____
_____

Images Or Drawing

Walk, Hike, Camp, & Sightseeing

Date: _____ Weather: _____

Start Time: _____ Time End: _____
Total Time: _____ Distance: _____
Elevation: _____
Walk/Hike Trail Type: _____

Rate The Walk/Hike/Camp ✿ ✿ ✿ ✿ ✿

City/State: _____
Trail Name/s: _____
Terrain: _____
Phone Reception: [YES | | NO]
First Visit ✿   Return Visit ✿

Companion/s: _____
_____

Bathroom? Water?: _____

Observances of Interest: _____
_____
_____
_____
_____

Things To Bring: _____
_____
_____

Notes For Next Time: _____
_____
_____

Notes & Journaling

_____
_____
_____
_____
_____
_____
_____
_____
_____
_____
_____
_____

Images Or Drawing

Walk, Hike, Camp, & Sightseeing

Date: _____   Weather: _____

Start Time: _____ Time End: _____
Total Time: _____ Distance: _____
Elevation: _____
Walk/Hike Trail Type: _____

Rate The Walk/Hike/Camp ✿ ✿ ✿ ✿ ✿

City/State: _____
Trail Name/s: _____
Terrain: _____
Phone Reception: | YES | | NO |
First Visit ✿   Return Visit ✿

Companion/s: _____

_____

Bathroom? Water?: _____

Observances of Interest: _____
_____
_____
_____
_____

Things To Bring: _____
_____
_____

Notes For Next Time: _____
_____
_____

Notes & Journaling

Images Or Drawing

Walk, Hike, Camp, & Sightseeing

Date: Weather:

Start Time: _____ Time End: _____
Total Time: _____ Distance: _____
Elevation: _____
Walk/Hike Trail Type: _____

Rate The Walk/Hike/Camp ✿ ✿ ✿ ✿ ✿

City/State: _____
Trail Name/s: _____
Terrain: _____
Phone Reception: | YES | NO |
First Visit ✿   Return Visit   ✿

Companion/s: _____
_____

Bathroom? Water?: _____

Observances of Interest: _____
_____
_____
_____
_____

Things To Bring: _____
_____
_____

Notes For Next Time: _____
_____
_____

Notes & Journaling

_____
_____
_____
_____
_____
_____
_____
_____
_____
_____
_____
_____

Images Or Drawing

Walk, Hike, Camp, & Sightseeing

Date: **Weather:**

Start Time: _____ Time End: _____
Total Time: _____ Distance: _____
Elevation: _____
Walk/Hike Trail Type: _____

Rate The Walk/Hike/Camp ✿ ✿ ✿ ✿ ✿

City/State: _____
Trail Name/s: _____
Terrain: _____
Phone Reception: | YES | | NO |
First Visit ✿ Return Visit ✿

Companion/s: _____

Bathroom? Water?: _____

Observances of Interest: _____
_____
_____
_____
_____

Things To Bring: _____
_____
_____

Notes For Next Time: _____
_____
_____

Notes & Journaling

_____

_____

_____

_____

_____

_____

_____

_____

_____

_____

_____

_____

_____

Images Or Drawing

Walk, Hike, Camp, & Sightseeing

Date: _____ Weather: _____

Start Time: _____ Time End: _____
Total Time: _____ Distance: _____
Elevation: _____
Walk/Hike Trail Type: _____

Rate The Walk/Hike/Camp ✿ ✿ ✿ ✿ ✿

City/State: _____
Trail Name/s: _____
Terrain: _____
Phone Reception: | YES | | NO |
First Visit ✿   Return Visit ✿

Companion/s: _____
_____

Bathroom? Water?: _____

Observances of Interest: _____
_____
_____
_____
_____

Things To Bring: _____
_____
_____

Notes For Next Time: _____
_____
_____

Notes & Journaling

Images Or Drawing

Walk, Hike, Camp, & Sightseeing

Date: _____ Weather: _____

Start Time: _____ Time End: _____
Total Time: _____ Distance: _____
Elevation: _____
Walk/Hike Trail Type: _____

Rate The Walk/Hike/Camp ✿ ✿ ✿ ✿ ✿

City/State: _____
Trail Name/s: _____
Terrain: _____
Phone Reception: | YES | | NO |
First Visit ✿   Return Visit ✿

Companion/s: _____
_____

Bathroom? Water?: _____

Observances of Interest: _____
_____
_____
_____
_____

Things To Bring: _____
_____
_____

Notes For Next Time: _____
_____
_____

Notes & Journaling

Images Or Drawing

Walk, Hike, Camp, & Sightseeing

Date: Weather:

Start Time: _____ Time End: _____
Total Time: _____ Distance: _____
Elevation: _____
Walk/Hike Trail Type: _____

Rate The Walk/Hike/Camp ✿ ✿ ✿ ✿ ✿

City/State: _____
Trail Name/s: _____
Terrain: _____
Phone Reception: | YES | NO |
First Visit ✿   Return Visit   ✿

Companion/s: _____
_____

Bathroom? Water?: _____

Observances of Interest: _____
_____
_____
_____
_____

Things To Bring: _____
_____
_____

Notes For Next Time: _____
_____
_____

Notes & Journaling

Images Or Drawing

Walk, Hike, Camp, & Sightseeing

Date: Weather:

Start Time: _____ Time End: _____
Total Time: _____ Distance: _____
Elevation: _____
Walk/Hike Trail Type: _____

Rate The Walk/Hike/Camp ✿ ✿ ✿ ✿ ✿

City/State: _____
Trail Name/s: _____
Terrain: _____
Phone Reception: | YES | NO |
First Visit ✿   Return Visit   ✿

Companion/s: _____
_____

Bathroom? Water?: _____

Observances of Interest: _____
_____
_____
_____
_____

Things To Bring: _____
_____
_____

Notes For Next Time: _____
_____
_____

Notes & Journaling

Images Or Drawing

Walk, Hike, Camp, & Sightseeing

Date: **Weather:**

Start Time: _____ Time End: _____
Total Time: _____ Distance: _____
Elevation: _____
Walk/Hike Trail Type: _____

Rate The Walk/Hike/Camp ✿ ✿ ✿ ✿ ✿

City/State: _____
Trail Name/s: _____
Terrain: _____
Phone Reception: | YES | | NO |
First Visit ✿   Return Visit ✿

Companion/s: _____
_____

Bathroom? Water?: _____

Observances of Interest: _____
_____
_____
_____
_____

Things To Bring: _____
_____
_____

Notes For Next Time: _____
_____
_____

Notes & Journaling

_____

_____

_____

_____

_____

_____

_____

_____

_____

_____

_____

_____

_____

Images Or Drawing

Walk, Hike, Camp, & Sightseeing

Date: Weather:

Start Time: _____Time End: _____
Total Time: _____Distance: _____
Elevation: _____
Walk/Hike Trail Type: _____

Rate The Walk/Hike/Camp ✿ ✿ ✿ ✿ ✿

City/State: _____
Trail Name/s: _____
Terrain: _____
Phone Reception: | YES | | NO |
First Visit ✿   Return Visit ✿

Companion/s: _____
_____

Bathroom? Water?: _____

Observances of Interest: _____
_____
_____
_____
_____

Things To Bring: _____
_____
_____

Notes For Next Time: _____
_____
_____

Notes & Journaling

Images Or Drawing

Walk, Hike, Camp, & Sightseeing

Date: Weather:

Start Time: _____ Time End: _____
Total Time: _____ Distance: _____
Elevation: _____
Walk/Hike Trail Type: _____

Rate The Walk/Hike/Camp ✿ ✿ ✿ ✿ ✿

City/State: _____
Trail Name/s: _____
Terrain: _____
Phone Reception: | YES | | NO |
First Visit ✿   Return Visit   ✿

Companion/s: _____
_____

Bathroom? Water?: _____

Observances of Interest: _____
_____
_____
_____
_____

Things To Bring: _____
_____
_____

Notes For Next Time: _____
_____
_____

Notes & Journaling

Images Or Drawing

Walk, Hike, Camp, & Sightseeing

Date: _____ Weather: _____

Start Time: _____ Time End: _____
Total Time: _____ Distance: _____
Elevation: _____
Walk/Hike Trail Type: _____

Rate The Walk/Hike/Camp ✿ ✿ ✿ ✿ ✿

City/State: _____
Trail Name/s: _____
Terrain: _____
Phone Reception: | YES | | NO |
First Visit ✿   Return Visit ✿

Companion/s: _____
_____

Bathroom? Water?: _____

Observances of Interest: _____
_____
_____
_____
_____

Things To Bring: _____
_____
_____

Notes For Next Time: _____
_____
_____

Notes & Journaling

Images Or Drawing

Walk, Hike, Camp, & Sightseeing

Date: _____ Weather: _____

Start Time: _____ Time End: _____
Total Time: _____ Distance: _____
Elevation: _____
Walk/Hike Trail Type: _____

Rate The Walk/Hike/Camp ✿ ✿ ✿ ✿ ✿

City/State: _____
Trail Name/s: _____
Terrain: _____
Phone Reception: | YES | | NO |
First Visit ✿   Return Visit ✿

Companion/s: _____
_____

Bathroom? Water?: _____

Observances of Interest: _____
_____
_____
_____
_____

Things To Bring: _____
_____
_____

Notes For Next Time: _____
_____
_____

Notes & Journaling

Images Or Drawing

Walk, Hike, Camp, & Sightseeing

Date: Weather:

Start Time: _____ Time End: _____
Total Time: _____ Distance: _____
Elevation: _____
Walk/Hike Trail Type: _____

Rate The Walk/Hike/Camp ✿ ✿ ✿ ✿ ✿

City/State: _____
Trail Name/s: _____
Terrain: _____
Phone Reception: | YES | | NO |
First Visit ✿   Return Visit ✿

Companion/s: _____
_____

Bathroom? Water?: _____

Observances of Interest: _____
_____
_____
_____
_____

Things To Bring: _____
_____
_____

Notes For Next Time: _____
_____
_____

Notes & Journaling

Images Or Drawing

Walk, Hike, Camp, & Sightseeing

Date: Weather:

Start Time: _____ Time End: _____
Total Time: _____ Distance: _____
Elevation: _____
Walk/Hike Trail Type: _____

Rate The Walk/Hike/Camp ✿ ✿ ✿ ✿ ✿

City/State: _____
Trail Name/s: _____
Terrain: _____
Phone Reception: | YES | | NO |
First Visit ✿   Return Visit ✿

Companion/s: _____

_____

Bathroom? Water?: _____

Observances of Interest: _____

_____
_____
_____
_____

Things To Bring: _____

_____
_____

Notes For Next Time: _____

_____
_____

Notes & Journaling

_____
_____
_____
_____
_____
_____
_____
_____
_____
_____
_____
_____
_____

Images Or Drawing

Walk, Hike, Camp, & Sightseeing

Date: Weather:

Start Time: _____Time End: _____
Total Time: _____Distance: _____
Elevation: _____
Walk/Hike Trail Type: _____

Rate The Walk/Hike/Camp ✿ ✿ ✿ ✿ ✿

City/State: _____
Trail Name/s: _____
Terrain: _____
Phone Reception: | YES | | NO |
First Visit ✿   Return Visit ✿

Companion/s: _____
_____

Bathroom? Water?: _____

Observances of Interest: _____
_____
_____
_____
_____

Things To Bring: _____
_____
_____

Notes For Next Time: _____
_____
_____

Notes & Journaling

Images Or Drawing

Walk, Hike, Camp, & Sightseeing

Date: _____ Weather: _____

Start Time: _____ Time End: _____
Total Time: _____ Distance: _____
Elevation: _____
Walk/Hike Trail Type: _____

Rate The Walk/Hike/Camp ✿ ✿ ✿ ✿ ✿

City/State: _____
Trail Name/s: _____
Terrain: _____
Phone Reception: | YES | | NO |
First Visit ✿   Return Visit ✿

Companion/s: _____

Bathroom? Water?: _____

Observances of Interest: _____
_____
_____
_____
_____

Things To Bring: _____
_____
_____

Notes For Next Time: _____
_____
_____

Notes & Journaling

_____
_____
_____
_____
_____
_____
_____
_____
_____
_____
_____
_____
_____

Images Or Drawing

Walk, Hike, Camp, & Sightseeing

Date: _____ Weather: _____

Start Time: _____ Time End: _____
Total Time: _____ Distance: _____
Elevation: _____
Walk/Hike Trail Type: _____

Rate The Walk/Hike/Camp ✿ ✿ ✿ ✿ ✿

City/State: _____
Trail Name/s: _____
Terrain: _____
Phone Reception: | YES | | NO |
First Visit ✿   Return Visit ✿

Companion/s: _____
_____

Bathroom? Water?: _____

Observances of Interest: _____
_____
_____
_____
_____

Things To Bring: _____
_____
_____

Notes For Next Time: _____
_____
_____

Notes & Journaling

_____
_____
_____
_____
_____
_____
_____
_____
_____
_____
_____
_____
_____

Images Or Drawing

Walk, Hike, Camp, & Sightseeing

Date: _____ Weather: _____

Start Time: _____ Time End: _____
Total Time: _____ Distance: _____
Elevation: _____
Walk/Hike Trail Type: _____

Rate The Walk/Hike/Camp ✿ ✿ ✿ ✿ ✿

City/State: _____
Trail Name/s: _____
Terrain: _____
Phone Reception: | YES | | NO |
First Visit ✿   Return Visit ✿

Companion/s: _____

_____

Bathroom? Water?: _____

Observances of Interest: _____

_____
_____
_____
_____

Things To Bring: _____

_____
_____

Notes For Next Time: _____

_____
_____

Notes & Journaling

_____
_____
_____
_____
_____
_____
_____
_____
_____
_____
_____
_____
_____

Images Or Drawing

Walk, Hike, Camp, & Sightseeing

Date: **Weather:**

Start Time: _____ Time End: _____

Total Time: _____ Distance: _____

Elevation: _____

Walk/Hike Trail Type: _____

Rate The Walk/Hike/Camp ✿ ✿ ✿ ✿ ✿

City/State: _____

Trail Name/s: _____

Terrain: _____

Phone Reception: | YES | | NO |

First Visit ✿   Return Visit ✿

Companion/s: _____

_____

Bathroom? Water?: _____

Observances of Interest: _____

_____

_____

_____

_____

Things To Bring: _____

_____

_____

Notes For Next Time: _____

_____

_____

Notes & Journaling

_____
_____
_____
_____
_____
_____
_____
_____
_____
_____
_____
_____
_____

Images Or Drawing

Walk, Hike, Camp, & Sightseeing

Date: Weather:

Start Time: _____ Time End: _____
Total Time: _____ Distance: _____
Elevation: _____
Walk/Hike Trail Type: _____

Rate The Walk/Hike/Camp ✿ ✿ ✿ ✿ ✿

City/State: _____
Trail Name/s: _____
Terrain: _____
Phone Reception: | YES | NO |
First Visit ✿   Return Visit   ✿

Companion/s: _____

Bathroom? Water?: _____

Observances of Interest: _____
_____
_____
_____
_____

Things To Bring: _____
_____

Notes For Next Time: _____
_____

Notes & Journaling

_____
_____
_____
_____
_____
_____
_____
_____
_____
_____
_____
_____

Images Or Drawing

Walk, Hike, Camp, & Sightseeing

Date: Weather:

Start Time: _____Time End: _____
Total Time: _____Distance: _____
Elevation: _____
Walk/Hike Trail Type: _____

Rate The Walk/Hike/Camp ✿ ✿ ✿ ✿ ✿

City/State: _____
Trail Name/s: _____
Terrain: _____
Phone Reception: | YES | | NO |
First Visit ✿   Return Visit   ✿

Companion/s: _____
_____

Bathroom? Water?: _____

Observances of Interest: _____
_____
_____
_____
_____

Things To Bring: _____
_____
_____

Notes For Next Time: _____
_____
_____

Notes & Journaling

_____
_____
_____
_____
_____
_____
_____
_____
_____
_____
_____
_____
_____

Images Or Drawing

Walk, Hike, Camp, & Sightseeing

Date: Weather:

Start Time: _____ Time End: _____
Total Time: _____ Distance: _____
Elevation: _____
Walk/Hike Trail Type: _____

Rate The Walk/Hike/Camp ✿ ✿ ✿ ✿ ✿

City/State: _____
Trail Name/s: _____
Terrain: _____
Phone Reception: | YES | | NO |
First Visit ✿   Return Visit   ✿

Companion/s: _____
_____

Bathroom? Water?: _____

Observances of Interest: _____
_____
_____
_____
_____

Things To Bring: _____
_____

Notes For Next Time: _____
_____
_____

Notes & Journaling

_____
_____
_____
_____
_____
_____
_____
_____
_____
_____
_____
_____
_____

Images Or Drawing

Walk, Hike, Camp, & Sightseeing

Date: Weather:

Start Time: _____ Time End: _____
Total Time: _____ Distance: _____
Elevation: _____
Walk/Hike Trail Type: _____

Rate The Walk/Hike/Camp ✿ ✿ ✿ ✿ ✿

City/State: _____
Trail Name/s: _____
Terrain: _____
Phone Reception: | YES | | NO |
First Visit ✿   Return Visit ✿

Companion/s: _____

_____

Bathroom? Water?: _____

Observances of Interest: _____

_____
_____
_____
_____

Things To Bring: _____

_____
_____

Notes For Next Time: _____

_____
_____

Notes & Journaling

_____
_____
_____
_____
_____
_____
_____
_____
_____
_____
_____
_____
_____

Images Or Drawing

Walk, Hike, Camp, & Sightseeing

Date: _____ Weather: _____

Start Time: _____Time End: _____
Total Time: _____Distance: _____
Elevation: _____
Walk/Hike Trail Type: _____

Rate The Walk/Hike/Camp ✿ ✿ ✿ ✿ ✿

City/State: _____
Trail Name/s: _____
Terrain: _____
Phone Reception: | YES | | NO |
First Visit ✿   Return Visit ✿

Companion/s: _____
_____

Bathroom? Water?: _____

Observances of Interest: _____
_____
_____
_____
_____

Things To Bring: _____
_____
_____

Notes For Next Time: _____
_____
_____

Notes & Journaling

_____
_____
_____
_____
_____
_____
_____
_____
_____
_____
_____
_____
_____

Images Or Drawing

Walk, Hike, Camp, & Sightseeing

Date: Weather:

Start Time: _____Time End: _____

Total Time: _____Distance: _____

Elevation: _____

Walk/Hike Trail Type: _____

Rate The Walk/Hike/Camp   ✿ ✿ ✿ ✿ ✿

City/State: _____

Trail Name/s: _____

Terrain: _____

Phone Reception: | YES | NO |

First Visit ✿   Return Visit   ✿

Companion/s: _____

_____

Bathroom? Water?: _____

Observances of Interest: _____

_____

_____

_____

_____

Things To Bring: _____

_____

Notes For Next Time: _____

_____

_____

Notes & Journaling

_____
_____
_____
_____
_____
_____
_____
_____
_____
_____
_____
_____
_____

Images Or Drawing

Walk, Hike, Camp, & Sightseeing

Date: Weather:

Start Time: _____Time End: _____
Total Time: _____Distance: _____
Elevation: _____
Walk/Hike Trail Type: _____

Rate The Walk/Hike/Camp ✿ ✿ ✿ ✿ ✿

City/State: _____
Trail Name/s: _____
Terrain: _____
Phone Reception: | YES | | NO |
First Visit ✿   Return Visit ✿

Companion/s: _____
_____

Bathroom? Water?: _____

Observances of Interest: _____
_____
_____
_____
_____

Things To Bring: _____
_____
_____

Notes For Next Time: _____
_____
_____

Notes & Journaling

_____
_____
_____
_____
_____
_____
_____
_____
_____
_____
_____
_____

Images Or Drawing

Walk, Hike, Camp, & Sightseeing

Date: Weather:

Start Time: _____ Time End: _____
Total Time: _____ Distance: _____
Elevation: _____
Walk/Hike Trail Type: _____

Rate The Walk/Hike/Camp ✿ ✿ ✿ ✿ ✿

City/State: _____
Trail Name/s: _____
Terrain: _____
Phone Reception: | YES | | NO |
First Visit ✿   Return Visit ✿

Companion/s: _____
_____

Bathroom? Water?: _____

Observances of Interest: _____
_____
_____
_____
_____

Things To Bring: _____
_____
_____

Notes For Next Time: _____
_____
_____

Notes & Journaling

Images Or Drawing

Walk, Hike, Camp, & Sightseeing

Date: _____ Weather: _____

Start Time: _____ Time End: _____
Total Time: _____ Distance: _____
Elevation: _____
Walk/Hike Trail Type: _____

Rate The Walk/Hike/Camp ✿ ✿ ✿ ✿ ✿

City/State: _____
Trail Name/s: _____
Terrain: _____
Phone Reception: | YES | | NO |
First Visit ✿   Return Visit ✿

Companion/s: _____
_____

Bathroom? Water?: _____

Observances of Interest: _____
_____
_____
_____
_____

Things To Bring: _____
_____
_____

Notes For Next Time: _____
_____
_____

Notes & Journaling

Images Or Drawing

Walk, Hike, Camp, & Sightseeing

Date: Weather:

Start Time: _____ Time End: _____
Total Time: _____ Distance: _____
Elevation: _____
Walk/Hike Trail Type: _____

Rate The Walk/Hike/Camp ✿ ✿ ✿ ✿ ✿

City/State: _____
Trail Name/s: _____
Terrain: _____
Phone Reception: | YES | | NO |
First Visit ✿   Return Visit ✿

Companion/s: _____
_____

Bathroom? Water?: _____

Observances of Interest: _____
_____
_____
_____
_____

Things To Bring: _____
_____
_____

Notes For Next Time: _____
_____
_____

Notes & Journaling

_____
_____
_____
_____
_____
_____
_____
_____
_____
_____
_____
_____
_____

Images Or Drawing

Walk, Hike, Camp, & Sightseeing

Date: Weather:

Start Time: _____ Time End: _____
Total Time: _____ Distance: _____
Elevation: _____
Walk/Hike Trail Type: _____

Rate The Walk/Hike/Camp ✿ ✿ ✿ ✿ ✿

City/State: _____
Trail Name/s: _____
Terrain: _____
Phone Reception: | YES | | NO |
First Visit ✿   Return Visit ✿

Companion/s: _____
_____

Bathroom? Water?: _____

Observances of Interest: _____
_____
_____
_____
_____

Things To Bring: _____
_____
_____

Notes For Next Time: _____
_____
_____

Notes & Journaling

Images Or Drawing

Walk, Hike, Camp, & Sightseeing

Date: Weather:

Start Time: _____ Time End: _____

Total Time: _____ Distance: _____

Elevation: _____

Walk/Hike Trail Type: _____

Rate The Walk/Hike/Camp ✿ ✿ ✿ ✿ ✿

City/State: _____

Trail Name/s: _____

Terrain: _____

Phone Reception: | YES | | NO |

First Visit ✿   Return Visit ✿

Companion/s: _____
_____

Bathroom? Water?: _____

Observances of Interest: _____
_____
_____
_____
_____

Things To Bring: _____
_____
_____

Notes For Next Time: _____
_____
_____

Notes & Journaling

_____
_____
_____
_____
_____
_____
_____
_____
_____
_____
_____
_____
_____

Images Or Drawing

Walk, Hike, Camp, & Sightseeing

Date: **Weather:**

Start Time: _____ **Time End:** _____
Total Time: _____ **Distance:** _____
Elevation: _____
Walk/Hike Trail Type: _____

Rate The Walk/Hike/Camp ✿ ✿ ✿ ✿ ✿

City/State: _____
Trail Name/s: _____
Terrain: _____
Phone Reception: | YES | | NO |
First Visit ✿   **Return Visit** ✿

Companion/s: _____
_____

Bathroom? Water?: _____

Observances of Interest: _____
_____
_____
_____
_____

Things To Bring: _____
_____
_____

Notes For Next Time: _____
_____
_____

Notes & Journaling

_____
_____
_____
_____
_____
_____
_____
_____
_____
_____
_____
_____
_____

Images Or Drawing

Walk, Hike, Camp, & Sightseeing

Date: Weather:

Start Time: _____ Time End: _____
Total Time: _____ Distance: _____
Elevation: _____
Walk/Hike Trail Type: _____

Rate The Walk/Hike/Camp ✿ ✿ ✿ ✿ ✿

City/State: _____
Trail Name/s: _____
Terrain: _____
Phone Reception: | YES | | NO |
First Visit ✿   Return Visit ✿

Companion/s: _____
_____

Bathroom? Water?: _____

Observances of Interest: _____
_____
_____
_____
_____

Things To Bring: _____
_____
_____

Notes For Next Time: _____
_____
_____

Notes & Journaling

Images Or Drawing

Made in the USA
Middletown, DE
20 October 2023

41127002R00071